ADIRONDACKS

ADIRON

VIEWS OF AN AMERICAN WILD

NDACKS

ERNESS *by* CARL E. HEILMAN II

Introduction by BILL McKIBBEN

RIZZOLI
NEW YORK

First published in the United States of America in 1999
by Rizzoli International Publications, Inc.
300 Park Avenue South
New York, NY 10010

ISBN (hardcover) 0-8478-2169-2
ISBN (paperback) 0-8478-2170-6
LC 98-68195

Designed by Pentagram
Printed and bound in Italy

When all the wilderness has been 'civilized'...
And all the wild animals made tame...
Where then, will the restless spirit,
Seek out new adventures and games?

Dedicated to the keepers of the wild places...

INTRODUCTION Once, years ago, a pilot friend of mine took me up for a day in his small plane to show me the Adirondacks. I've lived in this place most of my adult life, hiked hundreds of its trails, paddled its streams and lakes, but suddenly, thanks to his Cessna, I could step back far enough that the thousands of mosaic pieces merged into a vast picture. And here is what I saw. ∘ Rock, first. Though almost all the rock of the Adirondacks is covered with trees, its folds and bends and crenellations are obvious, especially when the leafy trees stand bare as they do for better than half the year. The High Peaks, near the park's center, punch up in a granite jumble of Haystacks and Nippletops, Giants and Whitefaces. But those aren't the only bulges: ripples and ridgelines run off in every direction. Above my house, in the south-central Adirondacks, we wheeled the plane and stared at dozens of ridges marching off into the unseen distance. My town, Johnsburg, has forty peaks over 2,500 feet—and only two of them have trails. It is simply vast, this park, bigger than Glacier, Grand Canyon, Yellowstone, and Yosemite combined. And at its base is this rock: schist, gneiss, gabbro, anorthosite, the limestone muds of some forgotten sea, glacier-carved. You can follow the folds of rock, like muscles

A cascade along Padanarum Road at the edge of the Lake George Wild Forest

7

on some Greek sculpture, because nothing interferes—in most places no roads, no houses. Just this unbroken upheaval of bent rock. o Water, second. Collecting in all the dimples of that rock, vast lakes and tiny ponds. Three thousand or more in all, and on this clear cold morning, mist rose off every one, or so it seemed. Already the ice was coming, water freezing into lace along the edges. The first snow falling, water turned to powder, accumulated over time. For a season it would insulate the bear in her den, amplify moonlight, muffle sound. But with the thaw it would slip down some seep into a stream too narrow to bear a name, and then on into one of the ponds or lakes. And then, finally, it would drain off the great dome of the Adirondacks, south along the swelling Hudson, north along the Saint Lawrence. o Lastly, on top of the rock and the water, there was life. Trees, most obviously—the great banks of hemlock and spruce, the tamaracks turned yellow along the marshy edges, the swamp maples holding a few last red leaves, the beeches shaking their browns, the pines regal on the point of every lake. From the air I could not see many animals, but they were easy to infer—the bloody spot on the ice that meant, doubtless, a whitetail followed by coyotes who dined and left, only to be followed by the ravens, the vultures. I could see the beaver dams with their sinuous curves on almost every stream, changing the topography every day of the year. o And once in a while we would fly over a town. Not often—there aren't many towns in the core of the Adirondacks. This is a region larger

Caribou moss, blueberries, and fall detail on a rocky outcrop

8

units in the north of the park. And so the state government rallied to the challenge once more, zoning all the private lands of the Adirondacks to prevent runaway development. In much of the region you need forty acres to build a home; on the timberlands clearcutting is banned. The restrictions, of course, have not been universally popular—many Adirondackers feel they have restricted economic development—but they are the crucial reason this place still feels different. They are the reason it hasn't turned entirely into a tourist colony, a second-home haven.   ○   The future of that balance, however, is not guaranteed. Many forces constantly threaten to shake it.   ○ Each front blowing in from the Midwest, for instance, carries a cargo of acid rain—as many as a quarter of the park's ponds and lakes have been sterilized. And each year brings warmer temperatures, here as around the globe; if we don't halt rapid climate change, these carefully protected forests will be wrecked before the next century is out, the trees unable to adapt to, in essence, a new latitude.   ○

Other threats are internal. Residents of the park have always been relatively poor—not compared to other parts of the rural East, but certainly to much of the rest of this rich suburban and urban state. Unemployment is stubbornly high; few industries choose to locate far from transportation corridors. And that poverty harms local institutions—the schools and clinics and churches that glue a community together. Conditions are grim enough that many of the local towns bid for the right to host penitentiaries that no one else

The wild shoreline of Lake Lila

wants; the Adirondacks and surrounding fringes are the gulag of the Empire State.   ❍   All that bleakness can harm the consensus that allows this balance between people and nature. The politics of resentment flare sometimes within the Blue Line, and people demand the overthrow of the zoning laws or the eradication of wilderness areas. More and more we try to overcome those problems with education, with local community development, with communication. But it is always hard in a vast, sparsely populated region without even a single daily newspaper to serve us all.   ❍   The most you can say—and it is more than you can say for almost any other spot in America—is that the Adirondacks greets the twenty-first century with none of its options foreclosed, with its future still unclear. It remains wilderness; it remains peopled; it remains the site of a great experiment about whether humans and nature can make their living in the same place. These photos chronicle that experiment—even when they show some wilderness vista, some lonely lake, they are showing a hidden and complex history and politics and economics. This is no mere wilderness; this is about the most interesting and valuable conservation story on the planet today.   ❍   There is no resident of the park more qualified to depict its tentative and beautiful balance than Carl Heilman. The first time I ever met him was one morning in mid-fall, hiking up Giant Mountain. My wife and I thought we'd gotten up pretty early—the mists were still hanging in Keene Valley. But we were no

Apple trees in full bloom in the Willsboro area

more than halfway up the lovely granite face of the mountain when a fit and bearded fellow came bounding by us on his way down, tripod in hand. It was only later that I figured out who it was, and deduced that he had been up high for the sunrise and now was descending to attend to other business. ○ Carl has helped all of us to see this place where we live, to understand what a privilege it is to spend our short years in this ancient and brand-new place. And now, with this book, he will reach many more, sharing a story that can be told with light and shadow and mist and sparkle and hue and tint much better than it can with words. ○ More than anything else, as these images make clear, the Adirondacks is a place of coexistence—that is our particular glory. We are logger, storekeeper, balsam, hemlock, miner, minister, bear, and beaver. Farmer, guide, otter, apple tree. Skier, doctor, mother, father, bus driver, owl. Hawk, vulture, chickadee. Skinny striped maple, straight-grained ash, lift operator, school teacher, student. We are lichen after rain, blackfly, wood duck, laugh-haunted loon. Brook trout, brown trout, uncle, aunt, peeling birch. Ranger, writer, painter, musician, scientist, waitress, sugar maple, mink, and marten. Coyote baying at December sunset, deer disappearing over scraper bank. Road crew, coach, midwife, fireman, boat-builder. Cattail, pickerel, waterlily, fern. White pine, red pine, wintergreen, raven. Husband, wife, mate, child, litter, pup, fawn, kit, fry, larvae, hatch. Alive, here, in the same place at the same time. Part of each other.

Cloud veil over the summit of Mt. Marcy on the first day of spring

WILD WATERWAYS

WILD WATERWAYS The wild Adirondack waters flow in an endless cycle from the mountains to the sea, regulated by the rain and melting snow, and the whims of wild beavers. Forming the headwaters of five major river basins in New York State, the Adirondack Park contains about 2,800 ponds and lakes, 600,000 acres of wetlands, and over 30,000 miles of streams and rivers, making it the greatest river system in North America. ∘ For centuries, Native Americans used the waterways to traverse the region in the warmer months, and eventually they became the main avenues for travel by early explorers, trappers, and settlers. At one time in the late 1800s and early 1900s, many of the trees cut from the denuded Adirondacks were floated down the major water routes to the sawmills and paper mills. Today, most of the luxuriant mountains, and wild, tree-lined shorelines show few signs of human intervention. ∘ Unchanged by the mists of time, the ever-flowing water provides a dynamic display of light, color, and sound. Ripples along the edges of ponds reflect the sun-drenched greens of summer, and in autumn, smooth tongues of water flowing in the rivers are gilded with brilliant hues of red, yellow, gold, and the intense blue of a cloudless fall sky. A winter lake may have black

Opposite: A remote, wild pond, with a backdrop of the High Peaks
Previous page: Sunrise on Lake Lila

ice that is so clear it provides a window to the world below, but most often it is a solid gray mass of bubbles, slush, and freezing rain. o Along gentle sections of a stream or river, water gurgles and bubbles around the rocks; while on steeper reaches, there is a whole symphony of sound as water gaily dances from rock to rock, forming rapids, eddies, and whirlpools of foam. Cascades of water fall gently over steep, rocky drops with a soft hiss, or tumble into deep pools of water with a deep, resonant pounding that is felt as much as it is heard. o The sounds of lakes and stillwaters are more dependent on the weather of the day. Sparkling blue water, softly lapping the sides of a canoe, or washing over shoreline rocks in a summer breeze, has a relaxing and hypnotizing effect; the beaching of wind-driven waves on a remote, sandy shoreline is a wild sight with a stimulating, rhythmic sound. o In the quiet of winter, frozen lakes and ponds produce a unique variety of sounds. After the water has chilled enough to start forming ice, a brisk north wind may ripple the thin, freshly formed shards, creating the tinkling sound of high-pitched chimes. Once the lake's surface is completely frozen, a combination of moderate near-freezing days and cold sub-zero nights begins a resounding process of expansion and contraction. o The first songs of the solid, but thin, layer of ice on a brisk December night are quite ethereal, with high-pitched zaps and twangs ricocheting through the ice from one end of the lake to the other. As the ice thickens, the pitch settles to a deep, resonating boom that reverberates from the lake bottom to the surrounding mountains. This phenomenon continues until the ice is

A bullfrog oversees his wild domain

insulated with a blanket of snow. o Nights spent along the water's edge are a special treat. Magnificent shoreline pines are silhouetted against a backdrop of mountains and stars. Owls call back and forth, and a bittern's chugging call resounds through an early summer night. Bullfrogs spontaneously enter into a throaty chorus with the warbling song of the loons; beavers busily attend to their work, building, repairing, and gathering branches for the coming winter, and occasionally warning of intruders with a cannonball splash of the tail. o As dawn approaches, misty spirits rise from the water and dance with the glimmering of the stars and crescent moon reflecting on the water. The first soft glow of light begins low on the horizon, then spreads to absorb each and every pinpoint of light from the heavens, until the sky is fully enveloped with the pastel blue of early morning. The mist soon becomes iridescent with the pink flush of sunrise that silhouettes wind-sculpted pines on nearby islands, and highlights the surrounding mountains. Fish rise in the quiet bays, making ever-widening circles on the surface of the water, and ducks lead their young in single file among the rushes and pickerel weed to forage for breakfast. o In the warmth of the rising sun, the fog lifts from the water. An eagle flies to its perch high in the tallest pine on the shore, while an osprey circles overhead, its keen eyes intent on the water below, ready to tuck and dive in a instant to grasp its prey. Heron leave their nests, in the skeleton pines, heading out to search for food for their young, and the deer retreat from the shoals to the shadows along the shoreline.

On the shoreline of Pharaoh Lake

The shoreline of Deer Pond in the central Adirondacks
Previous page: Falls and foliage on the East Branch of the Sacandaga River

A pair of mallards forage for food
Opposite: The three-sided lean-to, a traditional Adirondack icon

Dusk over Pine Pond
Previous page: Oseetah Lake in the Saranac Lake region

Water grasses and tree root detail on Garnet Lake
Opposite: Canoeing the backwater of a beaver dam along the outlet of Pharaoh Lake

34

First light over the outlet of Good Luck Mountain Pond in the southern Adirondacks
Previous page: Buttermilk Falls on the Raquette River near Long Lake

Newly formed ice on the outlet of Friends Lake
Opposite: First snowfall of the season at North Pond, near Hague

The West Branch of the Sacandaga River in the Silver Lake Wilderness
Previous page: Goose Pond in the Pharaoh Lake Wilderness, near Schroon Lake
Overleaf: The wild northeast shoreline of Lake George

ADIRONDACK FOOTHILLS

Spuytenduivel Brook in the Pharaoh Lake Wilderness
Previous page: Peaked Mountain reflected in a beaver pond in the Siamese Ponds Wilderness area

50

ADIRONDACK FOOTHILLS The foothills are a sea of rolling green hilltops, interspersed with occasional shimmering blue bodies of water. Long windswept ridges, crowned with soft evergreens, are home to the fox and bear, who venture onto the open ledges to feast on wild blueberries. Rocky crags provide homes for the falcons and eagles, and screech owls and pileated woodpeckers find homes in old snags. These verdant mountains and lush valleys are all about life, and about the continuity of change that creates a constant freshness here throughout the seasons of the year. ∘ In the springtime, the swelling valley streams cascade through rocky glens, and then calm in deep, trout-filled pools and flooded beaver flows. Amphibious creatures call for mates from the vernal pools, and efts and toads clamber about the spring beauties and trout lilies that carpet the sunny forest floor. Light-green fiddlehead ferns and crimson trillium rise through the mosses to greet the budding forest canopy. As the magenta and white blossoms of the painted trillium begin to fade, pink lady slippers bloom among the caribou moss and conifers at the edge of open rocky outcrops. ∘ Tall, stately pines tower above the forest canopy, shading the ferns and mosses from the heat of the intense summer sun. Throughout the complaisant days of late spring and summer, birds and mammals nurture their young, and the trees replenish their stores. Abundant wildflowers bloom throughout the forests and fields and rocky mountain outcrops. ● As the solitary call of the thrush fades from the chill of the late summer evenings, squirrels scurry about, caching their harvest of beech nuts and pine cones for the coming winter. The lively green leaves of summer begin to darken as the forest prepares for its finest display. Soon, brilliant scarlet and crimson colors embellish the red maples in the marsh. The color gradually works its way up from the edge of the wetlands and down from the mountaintops until whole hillsides are resplendent with an exquisite medley of colors. ● As the colors drop and fade on the forest floor, the days grow ever shorter. The noontime sun drops closer to the horizon, no longer sending enough warmth to repel the bite of the arctic winds and deep snows of winter. The cold soon settles in with a vengeance. On sub-zero days, freezing trees pop with a loud report, and partridge seek comfort under the surface of the insulating snow. Animals that aren't able to migrate hibernate peacefully, or group together for survival, awaiting the flowing sap and warm days of spring. ● Many people go to a favorite place in the foothills each year, seeking relaxation and peace. The footpaths here often lead to swimming holes and wild, trout-filled ponds, or rocky outcroppings and ledges with views of higher mountains off in the distance. Along these paths the constraints of civilization fall away, and the only sound is from the wind in the treetops, or the spring peepers at the water's edge.

A red eft wanders among the club moss and fallen leaves

Showy lady slipper in the southwestern corner of the Adirondacks
Opposite: Painted trillium growing among the virgin pines in Pine Orchard near Wells

A monarch butterfly on clover in a clearing near Brant Lake
Opposite: Sheep laurel covering the edges of a rocky outcrop on Crane Mountain
Previous page: Black Mountain, the Tongue Mountain Range, Pharaoh Lake, Pharaoh Mountain, and the Schroon Lake area from Treadway Mountain

Lake-effect snow clouds moving in at dawn, Blue Mountain

Early morning light on a blue heron rookery and abandoned beaver lodge
Opposite: A small brook along the trail to Buck Mountain in the Lake George Wild Forest

A panorama including Blue Mountain, the High Peaks, Indian Lake, Chimney Mountain, Gore Mountain, Lewey Lake, and the Lake Pleasant area, from Snowy Mountain

Shadbush blossoms and Second Lake of the Fulton Chain from the summit of Bald Peak
Opposite: Early springtime view west from Hadley Mountain
Previous page: Hadley Mountain summit

Early light on Peaked Mountain
Opposite: Sunrise from Treadway Mountain

Adirondack lean-to on Fishbrook Pond

Fawn in the Pharaoh Wilderness
Opposite: Mid-August in the Blue Mountain Lake area
Overleaf: Autumn light on Snowy Mountain from Watch Hill

ON THE EDGE OF WILDNESS

ON THE EDGE OF WILDNESS The Adirondack Park ... an expansive wilderness of lakes, mountains, rivers, and wetlands ... a stunning landscape of ever-changing shapes, colors, and textures ... a wild environment of varied habitats and weather extremes ... a unique patchwork of forever-wild state lands and privately owned working forests ... and, a diversified mix of farming towns, resort villages, and working communities where people co-exist with nature and wildness. ○ The quiet, rural towns and villages of the Adirondacks are nestled in the valleys among the mountains and foothills, or are situated along the waterways or at prominent crossroads. A few, like Lake George, Lake Placid, and Old Forge are resort communities that cater primarily to tourists. Other, larger towns, like Dannemora, Northville, Saranac Lake, Schroon Lake, Ticonderoga, Tupper Lake, and Warrensburg, have a mix of businesses that provide services for both local and seasonal residents. Practically every settlement in the park large enough to have a post office has its own volunteer fire company, a general store that can supply most of the staples for the surrounding community, and churches and organizations that help bind the community together. ○ Each of these small, tranquil villages has its own unique character

Opposite: Farm in the Friends Lake area
Previous page: Aerial view of Lake Placid village, the Olympic Center, the Lake Placid Club golf course, Mirror Lake, Lake Placid, and McKenzie, Moose, and Whiteface Mountains

and charm that come as much from the people who live there as from where the town is located. In the Champlain Valley, in the northeast corner of the park, towns like Willsboro, Westport, and Crown Point have grown up in the midst of rolling farm country. Here, panoramic hills of wheat, corn, and pasture often have backdrops of the higher Adirondack peaks to the west, and Lake Champlain and the Green Mountains to the east.   ◦   Keene Valley and Saint Huberts are situated along the picturesque Ausable River in a valley ringed by rugged peaks. The hamlet of Blue Mountain Lake is one of the smallest in the park. This quiet village lies on the southern shores of the attractive, island-studded waters of Blue Mountain Lake, with majestic Blue Mountain rising two thousand feet above the eastern shoreline. Like many of the other towns perched along the edge of a waterway, it is a serene and beautiful place.   ◦   Some of the smaller hamlets, like Cranberry Lake, Hoffmeister, Newcomb, and Santa Clara, are completely surrounded by wild mountains and lakes, and, until the train from Old Forge chugs through again, the rustic settlement of Beaver River, along Stillwater Reservoir, is accessible only by water. Most of the other villages in the Adirondack Park are connected by sparsely populated road corridors. In between these roadways lie vast areas of wildness, and many Adirondack residents only need to walk out their backdoor to be in the forest.   ◦   Most of the year-round residents who call this area home live a pace of life that is tied closely to the environment and the changing seasons. Both work and play are often dependent on the whims of Mother Nature. In a wild

A rural backyard in the southeastern Adirondacks

area like this, where weather systems blow in from the tropics in the summer and the arctic in the winter, and annual temperature extremes can range as much as 150 degrees, a person needs to adopt a creative and somewhat self-sufficient lifestyle. ❍ Much of the year here is spent working at ways to make it through the winter—both financially and physically. The annual cycle starts anew each spring, as the sun's warmth drives the mercury up above the freezing mark for whole days at a time, and the sap begins flowing in the maples. Holes are drilled, buckets hung, and downed wood from the sugarbush is used to boil the sap down to sweet syrup. ❍ As the fresh buds push out from the branches, and the last remnants of frost and snow melt from the earth, the quagmires of 'mud season' stop most motorized travel in the woods and on backcountry dirt roads. Shadbush trees soon bloom at the edge of the woods, signifying the beginning of black fly season—probably the least enjoyed annual event. As the ground dries and settles, it is time to till and plant the garden, hoping the full moon in June doesn't bring frost again this year.... ❍ Summer is a time for outside chores around the house and harvesting the garden, as well as a time to go fishing and camping, and enjoy the warmth of the sun. September frosts soon signal an end to the growing season and the beginning of hunting season and heating season. Time is often divided between building up the size of the woodpile and trying to put away some venison for the winter. Typically, the first flakes of snow fall sometime in October, but it is usually well into the gray days of November before the ground is fully covered with a blanket

Workhorses browsing on a frosty morning

of snow. ○ Shoveling sidewalks and roofs, plowing snow, thawing pipes, and carrying firewood are the chores of winter. Most often the cold January sun manages to warm the days to the mid-twenties, while nighttime temperatures range from the teens to well below zero. Fishermen's ice shanties abound on populated lakes, and some of the waterways and old roads become snowmobile routes. The wild forests are traversed by snowshoers and skiers, who look forward to an abundance of snow, and wish winter would never end. ○ Living in the region may have its rough times, but Adirondackers are a tough and independent breed, handy at adapting to many situations. While there are countless different reasons each person lives here, most appreciate the wild beauty of this region and the individuality and freedom they feel here—and they wouldn't trade the quality of this rugged existence on the edge of the wilderness for anything.

An abandoned hay rake in a meadow in the Brant Lake area

The Penfield Homestead Museum in the town of Ironville

Keene Valley Congregational Church
Opposite: Christmas decorations reflected in the Mill Pond in Brant Lake

A November morning along the shores of Brant Lake
Opposite: Frosty January days at Great Camp Sagamore
Previous page: Summer sunrise over Brant Lake

A panorama from Coon Mountain of Lake Champlain, the rolling hills and farms of the Westport area, and the backdrop of the High Peaks

96

Elsa checking out the chicken coop
Opposite: Sagamore Conference Center near Raquette Lake
Previous page: Asters, goldenrod, and joe-pye weed in a clearing near Santa Clara

THE BOREAL WILDERNESS

THE BOREAL WILDERNESS A transition zone between the prolific hardwood forests to the south and the wind-swept arctic tundra to the far north, the boreal regions are beautiful low-lying forests of larch, spruce, and pine, interspersed with glacial eskers that separate the ancient bogs from the seeps of water that drain the region. Most of the low-elevation boreal habitat is found in the northwestern quadrant of the Adirondack region, in the St. Regis and Oswegatchie River drainage basins, but there are also many smaller tracts of lowland bogs and boreal forests scattered throughout much of the Adirondack Park. Many of these wild reaches of sphagnous mosses, stunted trees, and boreal barrens have remained untouched and unspoiled since the last ice age. ∘ While the majestic peaks tower above the surrounding valleys with inspirational power, and the gentle waterways have a way of soothing the soul, there is a certain feeling of magic that comes from the forest cathedrals of the wild boreal regions. On a peaceful early-summer morning, the tall, slender spires of the balsam and spruce fade into the misty horizon of feathery larches, and lofty pines crown the meandering steep-sided eskers of glacial till. Gray jays and boreal chickadees call to one another while arctic woodpeckers

A pine-covered esker rises above the fog-shrouded boreal landscape
Previous page: A springtime festival of sheep laurel and larch growing on the mat of a kettlehole bog

search decaying trees for their breakfast. In the not-too-distant future, moose may once again be a common sight along some of the sandy shorelines. **o** At the edge of the water, on the buoyant sphagnum mat of the primeval bog, tiny orchids in varying shades of magenta and pink gently nod from side to side with the soft breath of the new day. Carnivorous sundews glisten in the morning light, each of their many tendrils adorned with a single viscous dewdrop. Older, purple-veined pitchers, half-filled with rainwater and digestive enzymes, rise from the acidic reddish moss. **o** The forest begins on the mosses of the floating bog. Trees progress in size from sporadic, stunted, mature growth that just barely rises above the tops of the cottongrass, to the much taller spires of conifer trees that stand firmly rooted on more solid ground. Various mosses cover the different soils, and ferns grow tall around decaying fallen timber. **o** When traversing one of these environmentally sensitive regions, travel gently and observe it from along the shoreline with a canoe to avoid trampling the easily damaged mat of the bog. At the Adirondack Park Visitors' Interpretive Center in Paul Smiths, a boardwalk along one of the trails allows close contact with a wild bog and boreal habitat. **o** These are enchanted regions that time has forgotten. A journey through the boreal wilderness is a trip back through the ages. It seems to take us back to a time before the hand of man weighed heavily upon the land, when bears, wolves, and panthers ruled this part of the continent, and glaciers still clung to the highest mountain summits.

Sundews and pitcher plants on the floating mat of a boreal bog

A wild boreal shoreline of balsam, larch, and spruce
Previous page: The boggy outflow of Chub Lake

Bog and larches at the outflow of Weller Pond
Opposite: Red maple and larch reflected in a kettlehole pond

Sphagnum moss and pitcher plants
Opposite: A November morning at the edge of a bog
Previous page: An untouched boreal forest

Soft light just before dawn
Opposite: Grass pink blossoms at the edge of a wilderness bog

118

The Oswegatchie River
Opposite: Cottongrass, balsams, and spruce, with conifer-covered peaks in the background
Previous page: An early morning fogbow and white-fringed orchis in the Fulton Chain area

Rose pogonia blossoms on a remote bog

The tannin-stained waters of the Jordan River
Opposite: The primeval feel of a wilderness bog

126

Rose pogonia, grass pink, cranberry, and pitcher plant blossoms

THE HIGHEST PEAKS

THE HIGHEST PEAKS The mountainous High Peaks region has some of the wildest and most rugged terrain found anywhere in the Adirondacks. From the alpine summit of Mt. Marcy, which rises a full mile above the level of Lake Champlain, to the remote wilderness of the Sewards and the Cold River area, this exceptional landscape encompasses a prodigious diversity of flora and fauna. ◦ Beautiful expanses of mixed hardwood and conifer forests grow in the sheltered, warmer valleys and on the lower flanks of the mountains' southern exposures. In spring these hardwoods embellish the mountains with the soft mint-green color of new leaves, and in the fall they fill the valleys with their warm radiance. A minor change in elevation or habitat is all that is needed, though, to replace the maples, beech, hemlock, and pines with an upper-elevation boreal forest that thrives in the colder climate of the higher peaks. These transitional conifer forests of balsam and spruce, mixed with a few birches and alders, grow in the thick carpet of mosses and ferns that covers the ancient rock of these mountains. ◦ Several of the highest summits rise well above the timberline and are home to an abundance of alpine flowers, sedges, and grasses that typically grow on rocky barrens a thousand miles

Heart Lake and Algonquin Peak from Mt. Jo
Previous page: East from Cascade Mountain

to the north. During their brief spring and summer, these plants must blossom, reseed the landscape, and grow, before they are once again encased in ice and frost for the other seven months of wintry conditions on these summits. ❍ There are many wondrous places in these mountains, some with evocative names that are as ethereal as the places themselves. Gothics is a remote mountain with steep, rocky flanks that conjures up thoughts of the finest cathedrals in the world. Tahawus–or Cloud-Splitter–the original and much more descriptive name for Mt. Marcy, gives a sense of the remoteness and elevation of this highest Adirondack summit. The Wolf Jaws extend along the east end of the Great Range with their jowl-like relief, and the furrowed edges of Sawteeth angle steeply into the depths of the Lower Ausable Lake. A rocky-tipped promontory of Nippletop Mountain enhances the spectacular panorama from Elk Lake, and the mountainous pile of rock called Haystack rises high above the wild glacial cirque of Panther Gorge. ❍ Lake Tear of the Clouds, a name that communicates both the delicateness and the ruggedness of the place, is a tiny gem of a lake perched in a small valley near the summits of Mts. Marcy and Skylight. The beautiful, crystal-clear waters that flow from this cold, spring-fed tarn, and over the ancient anorthosite and feldspar flumes and cascades of the charming Opalescent River, are the highest headwaters of the wild upper Hudson River. ❍ The beauty in these mountains is everywhere you look for it. It can be as simple as the pattern in the mosses and ferns and wind-rippled grasses, or as grand as the vista that sweeps from the rocks at your

Comet Hale-Bopp and the aurora borealis over Porter Mountain from The Brothers

The Dix Range from Round Mountain
Opposite: Clearing after the storm near Lake Tear of the Clouds

A morning view of the High Peaks from camp on an open ridge in the Hurricane Mountain Primitive Area
Opposite: The Dix Range and Nippletop from Noonmark Mountain

Beaver Meadow Falls
Opposite: Closed gentians grow in the endangered alpine habitat
Previous page: Dix, Dial, Nippletop, and Colvin Mountains, Sawteeth, Gothics, Armstrong Mountain, and the Wolf Jaws from Noonmark Mountain

155

The summit of Gothics
Opposite: Mt. Marcy, Mt. Colden, and Algonquin Peak from Gothics

Mt. Van Hoevenberg, Cascade and Porter Mountains, Big Slide Mountain, Yard Mountain, Mt. Colden, and Algonquin Peak from South Meadow

PHOTOGRAPHER'S NOTE

I use a variety of Nikon autofocus lenses for my Nikon N70, N2000, and FM cameras, ranging from a 20mm 2.8D wide-angle lens to an 80–200mm 2.8D zoom. I also use a Noblex 135U panoramic camera and Panolux exposure module. This camera uses a rotating 28mm lens to photograph a 140° wide view, and can be handheld or mounted on a tripod.

To enhance the colors and contrasts of some lighting conditions, I occasionally work with a selection of glass Singh-Ray filters, including a warming and enhancing polarizer, a warming filter, a color intensifier, and various graduated neutral-density filters.

In early 1998 I acquired a Roundshot Super 35 panoramic camera, which utilizes my fixed-focal length Nikon lenses and Singh-Ray filters. This computerized camera has a rotating head and will photograph any preprogrammed angle of view, including multiple rotations of 360°.

For best image clarity and color saturation. I mostly use slower-speed, fine-grain transparency film such as Kodachrome 25, Ektachrome E100SW, or Velvia.

ACKNOWLEDGMENTS

There are many people ... friends, family members, musicians, craftspeople, editors, educators, and fellow photographers, whose generous support and thoughts over the years have been inspirational. My enjoyment of nature first came from my parents, Carl and Alice, who fostered a deep respect and appreciation for the wild places on Earth. My sister, Mary Alice, and my children, Carl and Greta, provided me with many fresh perspectives on all aspects of life, and unwittingly became models on our forays into the wilds. And a very special heartfelt thank you to Meg ... wife, friend, mother, editor, partner, and special individual, who gave me the freedom to pursue my dreams.

Bill McKibben, author and friend, crafted an inspirational and thought-provoking introduction that communicates the essence of this grand, diversified landscape we call the Adirondacks. Bill Brown and the staff of the Adirondack Nature Conservancy, staff members of the Adirondack Mountain Club, Ray Masters of the Huntington Wildlife Forest, and Evelyn Greene have been invaluable resources for finding unique photographic opportunities. Thank you very much to everyone who has been involved with the production of this book. The wisdom and guidance of Megan McFarland and Publisher Solveig Williams at Rizzoli, and the soothing patience and imperceptible editing skills of Katherine Adzima, have made working with the folks at Rizzoli on my first book a memorable experience. John Klotnia of Pentagram, a designer extraordinaire, and Macarena Gutiérrez Eguía, magically transformed a collection of photographs and text into this evocative presentation.